Basketball
Outside Shooting

By Bill Van Gundy

BLUE ISLAND PUBLIC LIBRARY
BLUE ISLAND, ILLINOIS

Children's Press
A Division of Grolier Publishing
New York / London / Hong Kong / Sydney
Danbury, Connecticut

To Cin, Stan, and Jeff, for no matter what, always supporting and believing in me.

Book Design: Kim M. Sonsky
Contributing Editor: Mark Beyer

Photo Credits: p. 5 © Andy Lyons/All Sport; p. 6 © Brian Drake/SportsChrome; pp. 8, 10 (both), 12, 22, 23 (both), 26 (all), 28 (both), 30, 37, 41 (both) by Thaddeus Harden; p. 14 © Todd Warshaw/All Sport; p. 18 © Jeff Carlick/SportsChrome; pp. 20, 21 (both) by Debbie Moyer; p. 34 © Michael Zito/SportsChrome.

Visit Children's Press on the Internet at:
http://publishing.grolier.com

Library of Congress Cataloging-in-Publication Data

Van Gundy, Bill.
  Basketball : outside shooting / by Bill Van Gundy.
    p. cm.—(Sports clinic)
  Includes bibliographical references (p. 44) and index.
  Summary: Instructions and photographs show how to execute a jump shot in basketball, discussing how to prepare for and adjust the shot and how to practice shooting.
  ISBN 0-516-23363-7(lib. bdg.)—ISBN 0-516-23563-X (pbk.)
  1. Basketball—Offense—United States—Juvenile literature. [1. Basketball—Offense.] I. Title. II. Series.

GV889 .V33 2000
796.323'2—dc21
                                                                      99-058214

Copyright © 2000 by Rosen Book Works, Inc.
All rights reserved. Published simultaneously in Canada
Printed in the United States of America
1 2 3 4 5 6 7 8 9 10 R 05 04 03 02 01 00

CONTENTS

	Introduction	4
1	Your Shot Motion	7
2	Preparing to Shoot	19
3	Adjusting Your Shot	31
4	How to Practice	35
	New Words	43
	For Further Reading	44
	Resources	45
	Index	47
	About the Author	48

INTRODUCTION

Basketball players love to shoot. To them the prettiest sound in the world is the "swish" the ball makes as it falls through the net. Players are amazed by "outside" shots. An outside shot is any shot taken 15 feet (4.5 m) or farther from the basket.

    Shooters get the glory! They are highlighted on TV. They get a lot of newspaper ink. Also, they are often campus heroes. They are the stars. Some get playing time only because of their shooting ability. Coaches overlook their poor skills, such as defense or rebounding after missed shots. My son, Jeff, coaches the New York Knicks. The Knicks teams are built on defense. He says that at the end of close games he plays shooters, not defenders.

    I coached basketball for forty years. First I coached

The author of this book is the father of New York Knicks coach Jeff Van Gundy.

high school, then college. During those years as a coach, I learned that good outside shooters are made, not born. Practice is the key to being a good outside shooter. Repeating the correct motion helps you to make more baskets. Making more baskets will help you to succeed. Being successful will give you great confidence. Making more baskets, being successful, and having confidence all start with practice.

YOUR SHOT MOTION

It should be easy to make a shot. The basket is 18 inches wide. This is wide enough to fit two balls inside its rim. But in reality, it isn't easy to make a basket from the outside. Even in the NBA, players miss more shots than they make.

USING YOUR FEET, HANDS, AND LEGS

A good jump shot begins with your feet. Your feet should be shoulders' width apart. This is known as your stance. Your stance should feel comfortable to you because this is your base from which you jump on every shot. Your feet should share the weight of your body when you take a jump shot. The foot on the side of your shooting hand needs to be in front of the other foot. It also needs to point directly at

Figure 1: Point your forward foot at the basket.

the basket. [need photo of feet position figure 1].

When the feet are placed correctly, the shooter is what's known as "squared to the basket." This is very important to shooting success. The feet decide the line of the ball's flight. Many shots are missed to one side or the other because the feet are aligned incorrectly.

Once you are squared to the basket, bend your knees. Power for the shot comes from your legs when

Your Shot Motion

your knees are extended (pushed out). The longer the shot, the more you need to bend your knees. Don't dip the ball down trying to get more power into your shot. Instead, swing your shooting arm up until it is almost parallel to the floor. Your elbow will be flared away from your shoulder and shooting foot. Bend your elbow to form an "L." Your hand will point up and its palm will face the basket (See Figure 2, *p.10*). This hand is now in your "shooting pocket." Start every shot from here.

Now, bend your wrist back with your fingers spread to form a cup. The ball should be sitting on the pads of your fingers and thumb, but it should not touch your palm. The "V" formed by your thumb and index finger should point at the front of the rim (See Figure 3, *p.10*).

Your other hand (or "off" hand) should be placed on the side of the ball. The off hand doesn't help to shoot the ball, but it helps to guide the ball. Your two thumbs should form a "T." Make sure the off hand is not on top or in front of the ball. This will create a force against the flight of the ball.

BASKETBALL: OUTSIDE SHOOTING

Figure 2:
Keep the ball up with the palm of your shooting hand pointed at the basket.

Figure 3:
Bend your wrist back with your fingers spread to cup the ball.

Your Shot Motion

Don't forget about your head! Your head helps you to keep your balance during a shot. Keep your head still and directly over the midpoint between your feet. Focus your eyes only on the target (which should be the back of the rim). If you follow the ball in the air with your eyes, you have already lost the target.

Finding Your Shot

While practicing your shot, experiment to find the target that works best for you. You may like to aim at the front rim, the back rim, or the middle of the basket. You won't know which target works best for you until you try them all. Most good shooters use the back rim because it gives them a larger margin for error. Shots that are "long" may go off the board and in. "Short" shots have 9 inches (23 cm) of room for success.

Figure 4: Jump straight up for every shot.

Shooting

Start your shot by jumping, using both feet to extend your knees (See Figure 4). Feel how your body lifts off the floor. Always try to jump straight up. Try to get the same lift on every shot. Do not strain trying to jump higher.

Your Shot Motion

As you jump, start your arm action by extending your elbow. Push the ball "up and to" the basket, not straight out. When your elbow is fully extended (straight), snap your wrist forward and downward to release the ball. You should release the ball at the highest point of your jump. The ball should last touch your index and middle fingers. Think "up, over the rim, and in!" Your release is very important to outside shooting and is easy to practice.

After the ball leaves your fingertips, let your arm and hand continue their natural motion toward the basket. This is called the follow-through. When your follow-through is finished, your hand should point to the basket with the fingers pointed down (See Figure 5, p.14). Your guide hand should still be in the shooting pocket.

Continue to focus on the target. Watch for the ball to pass through the basket. If the ball doesn't go through the hoop but hits the rim or backboard, go after it! Offensive rebounds give your team another chance to score.

Your Shot Motion

THE THREE Cs OF GOOD SHOOTING

Along with a good shot motion, good shooters need to work on three things about their game: concentration, confidence, and consistency. Shooting is a head game. This means that you have to have your wits about you at all times. Slips in any of these areas will affect your shot and your game play.

Concentration

Defensive players try to distract outside shooters. A good shooter concentrates on what he is doing. A good shooter stays focused on the target, and his rhythm is unhurried.

Confidence

Coaches want their shooters to believe in themselves. Believing in yourself means that you have confidence. No matter what happened to the last shot, a good shooter believes that he will make the next shot. The great NBA star, Earvin "Magic" Johnson, once said, "If

Figure 5: Follow through on every shot.

BASKETBALL: OUTSIDE SHOOTING

Time Out!

Here are some tips that can help you make more jump shots:

- Make sure your feet are "squared" to the basket.
- Only shoot from within your range.
- Don't lean to one side or push backward as you jump.
- Push the ball "out" from the shooting pocket, not "up."
- Release the ball at the highest point of your jump.
- Make sure you snap your wrist to "follow through" on your shot.
- Don't move around while you shoot.

there was one part of my shooting that I didn't have in my early seasons, it was confidence." Magic worked hard to improve his shooting. Later in his career, he

Your Shot Motion

was a better shooter and a much more confident shooter. He also became a great shooter in the closing minutes of close games.

Consistency

To be a strong outside shooter your shot preparation and shot motion must be the same, time after time. This is called being consistent. You must treat each shot the same way. It doesn't matter whether a defender is guarding you closely or you are practicing on an empty court. Talking about shooting, Magic said, "Consistency is the key to good shooting. Every time I take a jumper, I want it to look like all other jumpers."

PREPARING TO SHOOT

The way you get ready to take each shot is important. This is called your shot preparation. How you prepare to take a shot is just as important to shooting success as the shot motion. You need to practice your shot preparation to become a consistent shooter. The key is to try to do everything the same way on every shot.

Magic Johnson stresses being prepared to shoot. "Great shooters all have one thing in common," he said. "They are always ready to shoot. When the ball comes to them, there's no hesitation."

THE "CATCH AND SHOOT" POSITION

Some defenses allow you to "catch and shoot" outside shots. This means that as soon as you catch a pass, you take a shot. Using the catch and shoot,

Earvin "Magic" Johnson was a great shooter for the Los Angeles Lakers. He worked hard on his shot preparation.

BASKETBALL: OUTSIDE SHOOTING

Figure 6: The "catch and shoot" position has three steps. First, take a step toward the basket with your non-shooting foot.

defenders can't disturb your shot. Here's how to have great success with this shot.

While waiting for the ball, square your body to the basket with your knees bent. Have your hands up and ready to catch the ball. When the pass comes to you, take the ball quickly to the shooting pocket and "step into the shot." First, step with your non-shooting foot so that you're moving toward the basket (See Figure 6). Next, bring the shooting foot in front to point at the

Preparing to Shoot

Figures 7 and 8: Bring the shooting foot in front so you're moving toward the basket. Jump straight up and take your shot.

basket (See Figure 7). Now you're squared up again and ready to shoot. Jump straight up and shoot using the shot motion you've practiced (See Figure 8). Make sure that you don't dip the ball or make any other unnecessary movements. This may throw your balance off and your shot will miss.

Sometimes a defender forces you to catch the ball

BASKETBALL: OUTSIDE SHOOTING

Figure 9:
When you catch a pass off a screen, stop on your inside foot.

when you're not squared up. Using good footwork can get you squared up. This often happens when coming off screens (when a player blocks a defender with his body) away from the ball. Keep your body low to the floor when coming off the screen so that your knees are bent. When you catch the pass, step hard on your inside foot to stop (See Figure 9). With

Preparing to Shoot

Figure 10: Pivot left or right to get your shooting foot in front and pointed to the basket.

Figures 11: Bend your knees and take the ball to the shooting pocket. Now shoot!

this foot anchored, pivot on either the ball or heel of your foot to get your shooting foot in front and pointed at the basket (See Figure 10). Keep your knees bent as you take the ball to the shooting pocket (See Figure 11).

BASKETBALL: OUTSIDE SHOOTING

Shooting off the Dribble

You will take most of your shots after you receive a pass. However, you must also be able to shoot "off the dribble." This means that while dribbling, you are able to stop quickly and shoot. Many players shoot better off the dribble than off the pass. Shooting off the dribble is how most players learned how to shoot while playing games on the playground. You dribbled the ball, then took your shot. Here's a way to shoot off the dribble that is sure to help you make more baskets.

Dribble straight toward the basket to within your range. Make your last dribble hard. This causes the ball to come up high so that you can take it to your shooting pocket easily and quickly. Stop running, put your weight on your non-shooting foot, and keep your knees bent. Step into the shot with your shooting foot pointed toward the basket.

Shooting off the Pivot

You know that once you stop your dribble, you can't

Preparing to Shoot

continue walking or running with the ball. If you do, you will be called for traveling by the referee or your playground opponent. However, when you stop your dribble you can use a pivot to change which way you face on the court. All you have to do to pivot is keep one foot against the ground and using the other, spin in either direction.

I teach players to always use their inside foot (the foot closest to the middle of the court) as their pivot foot (See Figure 12, p. 26). It can't be moved to step into the shot. As you pivot, bring the weak foot to its place to square up. (Many players will bring the weak foot too far forward. They will end up with their weak foot in front of their shooting foot. This disrupts the shooting action). Take the ball across your body to the shooting pocket (See Figure 13, p. 26). Now jump straight up and take the shot (See Figure 14, p. 26). Practice this until the motion becomes routine.

Some players use the same foot each time they pivot. It is always the weak foot. Why? This allows their shooting foot to always be free. However, I urge

BASKETBALL: OUTSIDE SHOOTING

Figure 12 (left): Use your inside foot (closest to middle of court) to pivot.

Figure 13 (below left): Take the ball across your body to the shooting pocket.

Figure 14 (below right): Jump straight up and shoot.

Preparing to Shoot

Time Out!

When getting ready to shoot, follow these simple rules:

1. Make sure your knees are bent before you want to jump.
2. Make sure your feet are squared to the basket with the shooting foot in front.
3. Make sure you take the ball to the shooting pocket for taking your shot.

my players to do whatever works best for them. The purpose is to put the ball in the basket. You don't get points for style.

Using a Fake

Forget about always getting "open" (unchallenged) looks at the basket against stubborn defenders. You have to learn how to "shake" a defender by using a

BASKETBALL: OUTSIDE SHOOTING

Figure 15: When your opponent comes at you, bring the ball up to the shooting pocket and fake a shot. This may get the defender to jump or lunge after the ball.

Figure 16: Now your opponent is out of position. Bring the ball across your chest and step in the direction you want to go. Now you can dribble past your opponent.

Preparing to Shoot

fake—making it look as if you're going to shoot, dribble, or pass. If your fake works, you'll be able to take your shot easily. One fake you can use is the shot fake. It should be a part of every player's shooting skills.

When the defender comes out to challenge your shot, get him off his feet or out of position. You can do this by quickly beginning only the arm action of your shot. Lift the ball to just above your eyes (See Figure 15, p. 28). When the defender reacts, swing the ball in the opposite direction that you want to start your dribble. Then quickly swing the ball back across your body at waist height. At the same time, step in the direction you want to go (this provides force). Step over the defender's foot to cut off his path to you (See Figure 16, p. 28). Take a hard, long dribble to create space between you and the defender. Now square up and shoot. It is important to keep your feet set and knees bent while lifting the ball. This keeps you balanced and able to move quickly.

THREE

ADJUSTING YOUR SHOT

To be a successful outside shooter, you must learn to be your own shooting coach. You have to know when your shooting motion feels too quick. You have to be able to see if your follow through is in line with the flight of the ball. To do this, you must study and know how your shot motion feels. You must know what causes you to miss shots. Only then are you able to change parts of your shot motion. This is called shot adjustment.

Don't panic if you miss a few shots. Everyone does. Make adjustments only if you continue to miss. Here are some causes of missed shots and tips on how to correct your shot motion:

Good shooters know how their shot motion "feels." When their motion is off, they can adjust.

BASKETBALL: OUTSIDE SHOOTING

When Your Shots Are Flying Long

Why? You're jumping forward rather than straight up.

Try This: Place pieces of tape on the floor to mark your takeoff place. You should land on the tape.

Why? You're hitting the wrong target.

Try This: Aim for the back of the rim.

Why? You're pushing the ball "out" from the shooting pocket rather than "up and to" the basket.

Try This: Be sure you pull back your wrist before you shoot, and check to be sure that your hand finishes up high.

When Your Shots Are Falling Short

Why? Your knees aren't bent enough to get the needed power.

Why? Your off hand is in front of or on top of the ball.

Why? You're aiming for the wrong target.

Adjusting Your Shot

Why?   You're pulling your shooting hand off the ball before completing the arm action and follow-through.

Why?   You're throwing your head back. This causes you to fall away from the basket.

When Your Shots Fall Right or Left of the Basket

Why?   You're falling to one side as you jump.

Try This: Place pieces of tape on the floor to mark your takeoff spot. You should land on the tape.

Why?   Your guide hand pushes on the ball.

Why?   The ball isn't sitting correctly on your shooting hand.

Try This: Check your elbow to see that it is in close to your body, not out wide.

Work on only one adjustment at a time. If you miss shots many different ways, begin by checking your stance. Your shot begins with your feet, so that is the first thing to check!

HOW TO PRACTICE

Good practices are planned around learning (or improving) a skill that meets your needs. Practices also should build on what you learned from the last practice. This will increase your variety of skills.

Start slowly and near the basket. Work first on your form. When your shooting motion is right each time, go faster and move farther from the basket. Move farther from the basket little by little. Work toward shooting at game speed. If you're practicing with a friend, take turns being the defender. This will help you learn how to shoot against defensive pressure. The defensive pressure you put on each other should be easy at first. Then slowly increase that pressure until you are both aggressively challenging each other's shots.

Practicing your shot helps you to become a better shooter.

BASKETBALL: OUTSIDE SHOOTING

There are many shooting drills that you can use. Try these drills, which have worked for players on every level:

Drill #1: The Release

1. Stand closely in front of the basket. Hold the ball above your head in the shooting hand with your wrist cocked. Your off hand may be up but not on the ball.
2. Concentrate on the target.
3. Fully extend your elbow to push the ball up, then snap your wrist to release the ball and follow through.
4. Focus on the target until the ball is in the net (See Figure 17).

Make a set number of shots from in front and to each side of the basket. Increase the distance only as you make almost every shot. Work your way up to the free-throw line by increasing the power produced by bending your knees.

Figure 17: Look at how this shooter has his eyes on the target as the ball is released from his hand.

BASKETBALL: OUTSIDE SHOOTING

Drill #2: Step In and Shoot

1. Begin by standing on the baseline 15 to 18 feet (4.5 m to 5 m) away from and facing the basket.
2. Hold the ball in your shooting pocket.
3. Your shooting foot should be slightly behind your pivot (weak) foot. Keep your knees bent.
4. Step in with your shooting foot to square up and shoot.

Move to different spots on the court within your range. Watch and mentally record where each missed shot hits. This information will be important when you need to make adjustments. Extend your range when you can regularly make 60 percent (six out of ten shots) of your attempts.

Drill #3: Off the Dribble

1. Begin by standing on the baseline 15 to 18 feet (4.5 m to 5 m) away from the

How to Practice

basket facing the mid-court line.
2. Hold the ball in a "triple threat" position.
3. Using your outside hand, take two dribbles in one direction or the other.
4. Stop hard on your inside foot. Pick up the ball off the dribble and take it to the shooting pocket.
5. Pivot on your inside foot to square up and shoot. Again, you want to use a reverse pivot on the outside foot.
6. Quickly retrieve the ball. Don't walk, run! Try to get as much exercise as you can.
7. Repeat the drill.

Change your starting spot often. Practice going to your left and your right. Remember to work on dribbling with your weak hand. Move farther from the basket when you begin to make 60 percent (six out of ten) of your shots.

This drill also can be done using a shot fake before taking the dribbles. Have a friend play defense. If

BASKETBALL: OUTSIDE SHOOTING

there is no one to practice with, use a chair or a cone in place of a defender.

Drill #4: Pitino

If you have a friend to practice with you, this is a great drill. I call it the Pitino drill because I got it from Rick Pitino when he coached at Providence College.

1. The shooter stands on the perimeter with his feet squared to the basket, his hands up and ready to catch the ball.
2. The defender begins by standing under the basket holding the ball.
3. The defender passes the ball to the shooter and "closes out" (rushes toward the shooter) to contest the shot, yelling at the shooter to try to break his concentration (See Figures 18 and 19, p. 41).
4. The shooter catches the ball, steps in, and shoots the ball.

Figure 18: Practicing with a friend is a great way to learn how to shoot against a defender.

Figure 19: When the defender passes the ball to the shooter, he should rush the shooter to contest the shot.

BASKETBALL: OUTSIDE SHOOTING

5. The defender stays on the perimeter to become the shooter.
6. The shooter retrieves the ball and becomes the defender.
7. Shoot from a different spot after each player has taken a shot.

When practicing hard, you will get tired. At that point, shoot a few free throws to cool down. Then continue your planned practice.

Once your shot has been mastered, you must use that same stroke in games. Many things can affect a shooter's performance in a game. A strong defense can make you hurry your shots. The crowd noise might disrupt your concentration. You might even be playing injured. Sometimes, the hardest hurdle to overcome is yourself. You must be relaxed, confident, and disciplined. Take only the shots you know you have the best chance to make. Remember, practice is the key to shooting success!

consistency doing something the same way each time

follow-through the shooting arm and hand action after the release of the ball

outside hand the pass receiver's hand that is farther away from the defender

pivot foot the foot that is stationary while the body rotates

shooting pocket the place from where a shot begins, 8 to 12 inches (20 to 30 cm) in front of the shoulder on the shooting hand side of the body

square up the body is directly in line with the basket and the front foot is pointed directly at the front rim

strong hand (or foot) the controlling hand or foot, such as the hand with which you write

target the spot at which the shooter aims the ball

triple threat position the ball handler has the ball in front of his shooting shoulder and is in position to shoot, drive, or pass

weak hand (or foot) the hand or foot on the side opposite the shooting hand

FURTHER READING

Goldstein, Sidney. *The Basketball Shooting Guide.* Philadelphia: Golden Aura, 1998.

Lieberman-Cline, Nancy, et al. *Basketball for Women: Becoming a Complete Player.* Champaign, IL: Human Kinetics, 1995.

McCarthy, Jr., John P. *Youth Basketball, 2nd ed.* Cincinnati, OH: Betterway Books, 1996.

Mikes, Jay, and Ray Meyer. *Basketball FundaMENTALS: A Complete Mental Training Guide.* Champaign, IL: Human Kinetics, 1995.

Stewart, Mark. *Basketball: A History of Hoops.* Danbury, CT: Franklin Watts, 1998.

American Youth Basketball Tour
http://www.aybtour.com
2150 Anderson SE
E. Grand Rapids, MI 49506
(800) 685-7194 ext. 6762

Web Sites
Women's National Basketball Association
http://wnba.com/
Get all the breaking news of the Women's National Basketball Association at this site. There are also player profiles available for you to research, and playing tips from the pros.

National Basketball Association
http://nba.com/
The National Basketball Association's own Web site gives you up-to-the-minute news about all things having to do with the NBA. Included are news articles that offer fans detailed reports about the teams and players around the league.

BASKETBALL: OUTSIDE SHOOTING

National College Athletic Association
http://ncaa.org/
Find school team schedules and view stats of your favorite teams and players. The NCAA online site is not just for fans, though. Learn about college basketball scholarship awards!

INDEX

B
backboard, 13

C
catch and shoot, 19–21
closing out, 40
concentration, 15, 36, 42
confidence, 5, 15–17, 42
consistency, 17, 19

D
defensive pressure, 35
dribbling, 24, 25, 29, 38, 39
drills, 36–42

F
fake, 29
finding your shot, 11
follow-through, 13, 16, 33, 36
footwork, 22

J
Johnson, Magic, 15–17, 19

N
NBA, 7, 15

O
off hand, 9, 32
off the dribble, 24, 38
off the pass, 24
offensive rebound, 13
outside hand, 39

P
Pitino drill, 40
pivot foot, 25, 38

S
screens, 22
shake, 27
shooting arm, 9
shooting foot, 9, 20, 23–25, 38
shooting hand, 7, 33, 36
shooting pocket, 9, 16, 23–25, 32, 38, 39
shot adjustment, 31–33
shot fake, 29
shot motion, 7, 17, 19, 21, 31, 35

BASKETBALL: OUTSIDE SHOOTING

shot preparation, 17, 19
square up, 8, 16, 20–22, 25, 29, 39, 40
stance, 7, 33

T

target, 11, 32, 36
Three Cs, 15
traveling, 25
triple threat position, 39

W

weak hand, 39
weak foot, 25, 38

About the Author

Bill Van Gundy has coached on the high school and college levels for 41 years. His teams are known for their aggressive man-to-man defense and disciplined offense; he frequently speaks at clinics and summer camps and has had 15 articles published. Coach Van Gundy is the father of Stan, the assistant head coach of the Miami Heat, and Jeff, the head coach of the New York Knickerbockers.